THE GUITAR CHORD CASEBOOK

by **Dave Rubin** and **Matt Scharfglass**

Table of Contents

Project Managers: Aaron Stang and Dave Rubin
Project Coordinator: Yoni Leviatan
Book Art Design: Carmen Fortunato
Technical Editor: Albert Nigro
Engraver: Mark Ralston

© 2000 ALFRED PUBLISHING CO., INC.
All Rights Reserved

Any duplication, adaptation or arrangement of the compositions
contained in this collection requires the written consent of the Publisher.
No part of this book may be photocopied or reproduced in any way without permission.
Unauthorized uses are an infringement of the U.S. Copyright Act and are punishable by law.

Introduction

Jimi Hendrix once said, "Learn your chords and everything else will follow." Though he was not the first to offer that sage advice, he certainly practiced what he preached. Jimi was a master rhythm guitarist who learned the right chords through years of playing experience.

The right chords. That is part of the secret to becoming a great guitarist. There are literally *thousands* of chords that can be played up and down the fingerboard, but what you need to know are the best and most useful. This book is your guide to that inside knowledge.

The 11 most essential chord types are pictured in grids starting in C and continuing through all 12 keys. Open chords, barre chords and hip four-note voicings are presented, giving you a choice of fingerings and location on the neck, for a total of 48 voicings in each key.

Whether you play rock, blues, jazz, country or any other style of guitar music, the correct chord information is contained within. By keeping this handy chord guide in your gig bag or guitar case, you will always have the chord form you need, when you need it, to sound great in any situation.

How to Use This Book

- Chords found within the first five frets do not have a fret number.
- X's indicate strings to be muted or not strummed.
- O's indicate open strings to be strummed.
- A box around a note identifies it as the root.

- The numbers under the grids indicate fingerings 1=index, 2=middle, 3=ring, 4 =pinky.
- An arched line indicates a barre, usually with the index finger.

- A barre below other indicated fingers is usually played with the ring finger.

Basic Chord Theory

Chords are derived from *chord formulas*. If that gives you a vision of a scientist working in a dark laboratory on something mysterious and beyond your grasp, you can relax. Chord formulas are founded on the simplest of math principles. If you can count to eight, and by extension 13, you can understand basic chord theory.

Chords are constructed from the major scale, also called the diatonic scale or Ionian mode. This is the "do-re-mi" scale we all know. Every key (there are 12) has its own major scale consisting of eight notes. Each note is given a number. These numbers are referred to as scale degrees. Shown below is the C major scale with the scale degrees underneath. The first note (1) is usually called the root, with the succeeding notes known as the 2nd, 3rd, 4th, 5th, 6th, 7th and octave (the same note as the root, one octave higher).

C	D	E	F	G	A	B	C
1	2	3	4	5	6	7	8

By combining various combinations of notes from the major scale, we create chords. Listed below are the formulas for the 11 chords diagrammed in each key. Keep in mind the following points as you go through the list:

- ♭ = lower that note by one fret.
  ♯ = raise that note by one fret.
  Ex: ♭3rd. In the key of C you would lower E to E♭.
- The notes repeat, in the same order, past the octave up to 13. Ex: C9. If you count past the octave (C), the next note, D, is the 9th note.
- Many chords double and even triple some of the notes from the formula for a fuller sound. Ex: A major barre chord may have three root notes. Likewise, some chords with more than four notes (13th) are often played without certain notes (5th, 7th, 9th) to make the fingering easier.

major = 1, 3, 5
minor = 1, ♭3, 5
dominant 7 = 1, 3, 5, ♭7
major 7 = 1, 3, 5, 7
minor 7 = 1, ♭3, 5, ♭7
9th = 1, 3, 5, 7, 9
13th = 1, 3, 5, 7, 9, 13
6th = 1, 3, 5, 6
sus 4 (suspended 4th) = 1, 4, 5
augmented = 1, 3, ♯5
diminished 7 = 1, ♭3, ♭5, ♭♭7 (6)

The 12 Major Scales

C	D	E	F	G	A	B	C
D♭	E♭	F	G♭	A♭	B♭	C	D♭
D	E	F♯	G	A	B	C♯	D
E♭	F	G	A♭	B♭	C	D	E♭
E	F♯	G♯	A	B	C♯	D♯	E
F	G	A	B♭	C	D	E	F
G♭	A♭	B♭	C♭	D♭	E♭	F	G♭
G	A	B	C	D	E	F♯	G
A♭	B♭	C	D♭	E♭	F	G	A♭
A	B	C♯	D	E	F♯	G♯	A
B♭	C	D	E♭	F	G	A	B♭
B	C♯	D♯	E	F♯	G♯	A♯	B

The Notes on the Fingerboard

Fret	E	A	D	G	B	E
1	F	A#	D#	G#	C	F
2	F#	B	E	A	C#	F#
3	G	C	F	A#	D	G
4	G#	C#	F#	B	D#	G#
5	A	D	G	C	E	A
6	A#	D#	G#	C#	F	A#
7	B	E	A	D	F#	B
8	C	F	A#	D#	G	C
9	C#	F#	B	E	G#	C#
10	D	G	C	F	A	D
11	D#	G#	C#	F#	A#	D#
12	E	A	D	G	B	E
13	F	A#	D#	G#	C	F
14	F#	B	E	A	C#	F#
15	G	C	F	A#	D	G
16	G#	C#	F#	B	D#	G#
17	A	D	G	C	E	A
18	A#	D#	G#	C#	F	A#

Hints for Choosing the Right Chords

One of the joys of playing the guitar is the nearly infinite number of ways to combine chords. But, like choosing your words, if you do it carefully you will be able to express yourself with confidence. As with good grammar, there are certain guidelines that will help you in crafting flowing, harmonious musical statements.

Open Chords

A simple but sure-fire concept is the use of open chords with their ringing open strings to maintain *continuity* in a progression. This can be particularly effective when the lowest open string is the root of each chord.

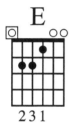
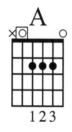

Common Tones

Combining chords that share some of the same notes (common tones) makes for fluid transitions.

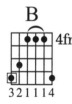

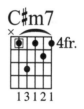
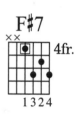

Bass Notes

Keeping the bass note of each chord on the same string and close together can make it sound as if a bass is accompanying you.

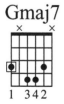

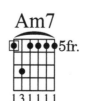
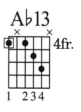

Key of C

C major

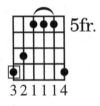

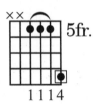

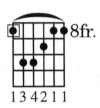

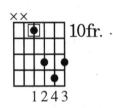

C minor

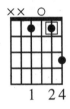

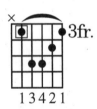

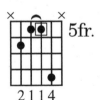

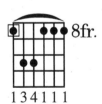

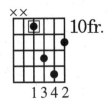

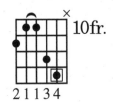

C dominant 7

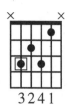

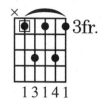

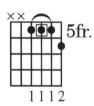

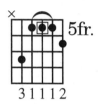

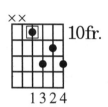

C major 7

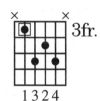

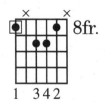

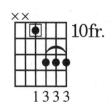

C minor 7

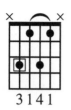

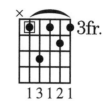

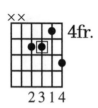

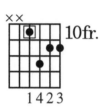

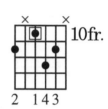

C9

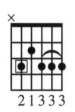

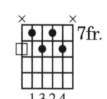

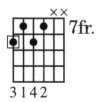

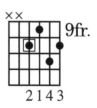

C13

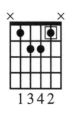

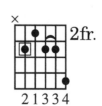

(C13)

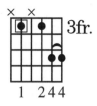 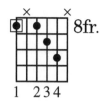

C6

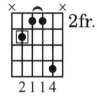 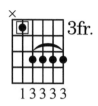

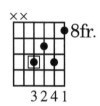

C sus

C augmented

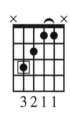 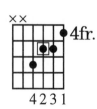

C diminished 7

 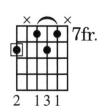

Key of D♭

D♭ major

4 3 1 2 1

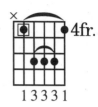
4fr.
1 3 3 3 1

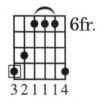
6fr.
3 2 1 1 1 4

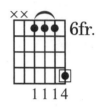
6fr.
1 1 1 4

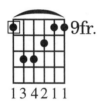
9fr.
1 3 4 2 1 1

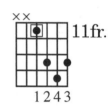
11fr.
1 2 4 3

D♭ minor

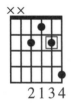
2 1 3 4

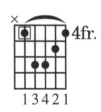
4fr.
1 3 4 2 1

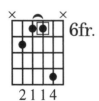
6fr.
2 1 1 4

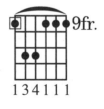
9fr.
1 3 4 1 1 1

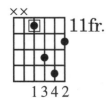
11fr.
1 3 4 2

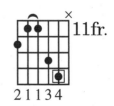
11fr.
2 1 1 3 4

12

D♭ dominant 7

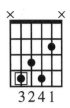

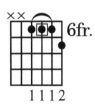
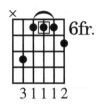

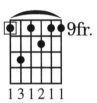
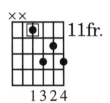

D♭ major 7

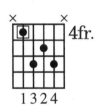

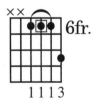
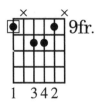

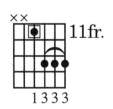

D♭ minor 7

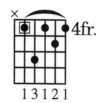

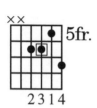

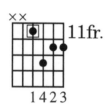

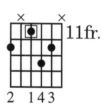

D♭9

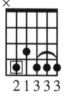

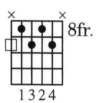

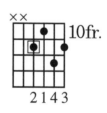

D♭13

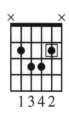

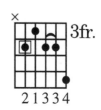

(D♭13)

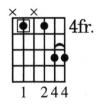 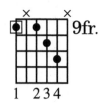

D♭6

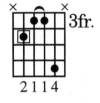 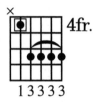

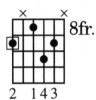 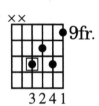

D♭ sus

D♭ augmented

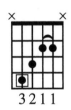 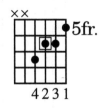

D♭ diminished 7

 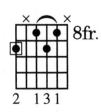

Key of D

D major

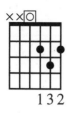
1 3 2

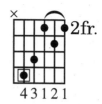
2fr.
4 3 1 2 1

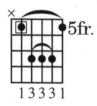
5fr.
1 3 3 3 1

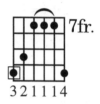
7fr.
3 2 1 1 1 4

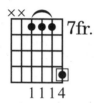
7fr.
1 1 1 4

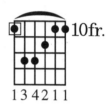
10fr.
1 3 4 2 1 1

D minor

2 3 1

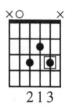
2 1 3

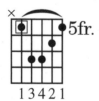
5fr.
1 3 4 2 1

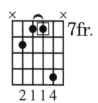
7fr.
2 1 1 4

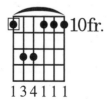
10fr.
1 3 4 1 1 1

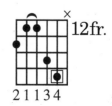
12fr.
2 1 1 3 4

16

D dominant 7

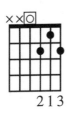

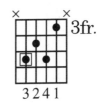

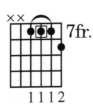

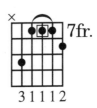

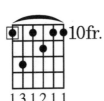

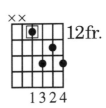

D major 7

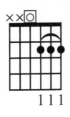

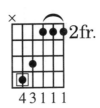

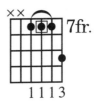

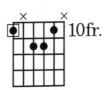

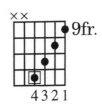

D minor 7

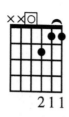 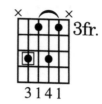

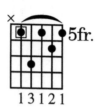 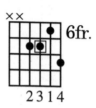

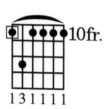 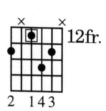

D9

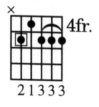 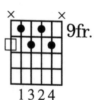

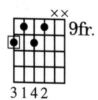 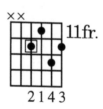

D13

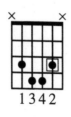 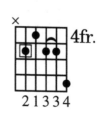

(D13)

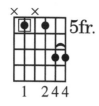 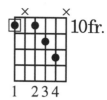

D6

 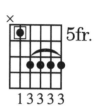

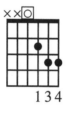 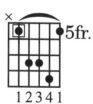

D sus

 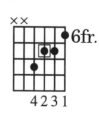

D augmented

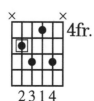 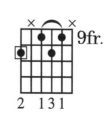

D diminished 7

 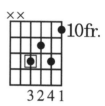

19

Key of E♭

E♭ major

1 2 4 3

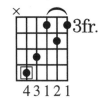
3fr.
4 3 1 2 1

6fr.
1 3 3 3 1

8fr.
3 2 1 1 1 4

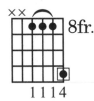
8fr.
1 1 1 4

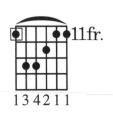
11fr.
1 3 4 2 1 1

E♭ minor

1 3 4 2

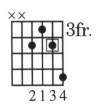
3fr.
2 1 3 4

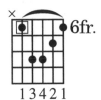
6fr.
1 3 4 2 1

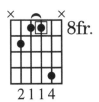
8fr.
2 1 1 4

11fr.
1 3 4 1 1 1

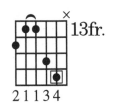
13fr.
2 1 1 3 4

E♭ dominant 7

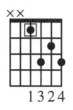

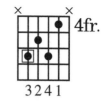

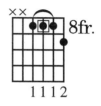

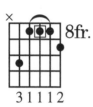

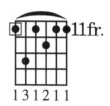

E♭ major 7

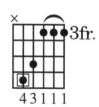

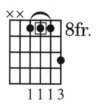

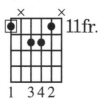

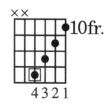

E♭ minor 7

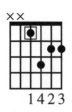
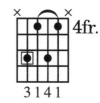

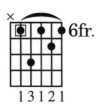
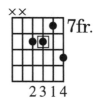

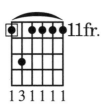
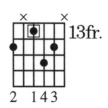

E♭9

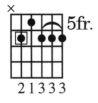
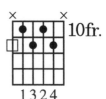

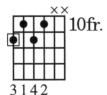
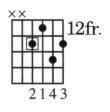

E♭13

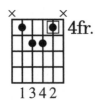
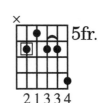

(E♭13)

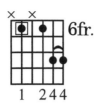 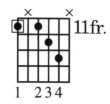

E♭6

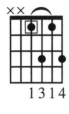 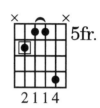

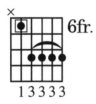 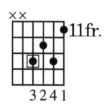

E♭ sus

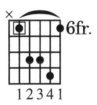 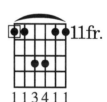

E♭ augmented

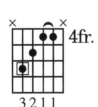 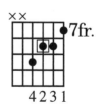

E♭ diminished 7

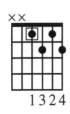 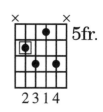

23

Key of E

E major

2 3 1

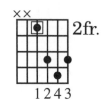

2fr.

1 2 4 3

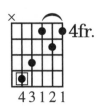

4fr.

4 3 1 2 1

7fr.

1 3 3 3 1

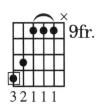

9fr.

3 2 1 1 1

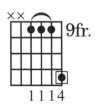

9fr.

1 1 1 4

E minor

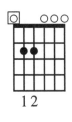

1 2

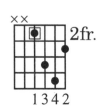

2fr.

1 3 4 2

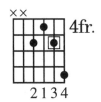

4fr.

2 1 3 4

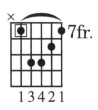

7fr.

1 3 4 2 1

9fr.

2 1 1 4

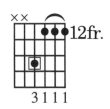

12fr.

3 1 1 1

24

E dominant 7

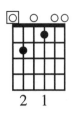 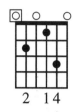

 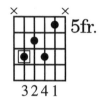

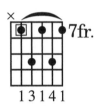 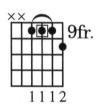

E major 7

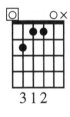 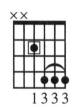

 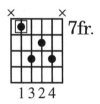

 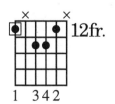

E minor 7

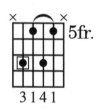

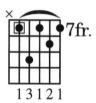

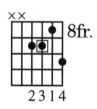

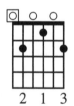

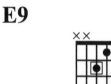

E9

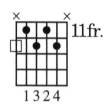

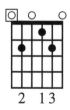

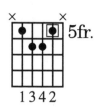

E13

(E13)

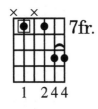 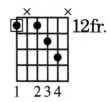

E6

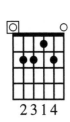 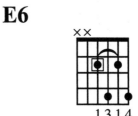

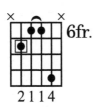 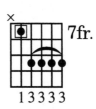

E sus

 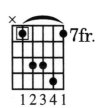

E augmented

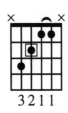 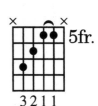

E diminished 7

 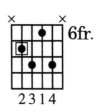

Key of F

F major

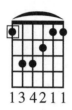
1 3 4 2 1 1

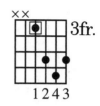
3fr.
1 2 4 3

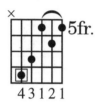
5fr.
4 3 1 2 1

8fr.
1 3 3 3 1

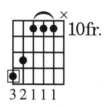
10fr.
3 2 1 1 1

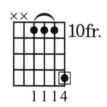
10fr.
1 1 1 4

F minor

1 3 4 1 1 1

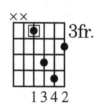
3fr.
1 3 4 2

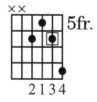
5fr.
2 1 3 4

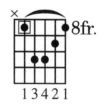
8fr.
1 3 4 2 1

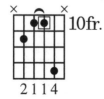
10fr.
2 1 1 4

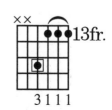
13fr.
3 1 1 1

F dominant 7

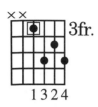 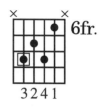

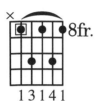 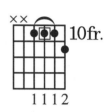

F major 7

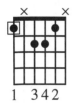 

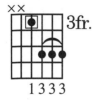 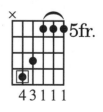

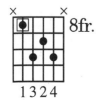 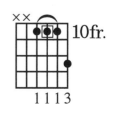

F minor 7

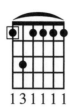
1 3 1 1 1 1

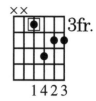
3fr.
1 4 2 3

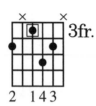
3fr.
2 1 4 3

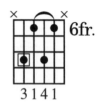
6fr.
3 1 4 1

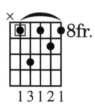
8fr.
1 3 1 2 1

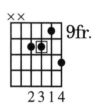
9fr.
2 3 1 4

F9

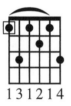
1 3 1 2 1 4

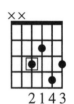
2 1 4 3

7fr.
2 1 3 3 3

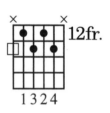
12fr.
1 3 2 4

F13

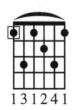
1 3 1 2 4 1

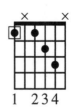
1 2 3 4

(F13)

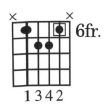 6fr. 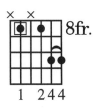 8fr.

F6

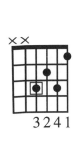 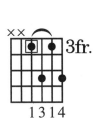 3fr.

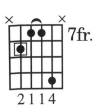 7fr. 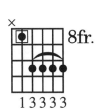 8fr.

F sus

 8fr.

F augmented

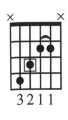 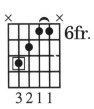 6fr.

F diminished 7

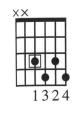 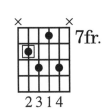 7fr.

31

Key of G♭

G♭ major

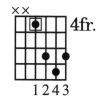

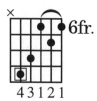

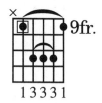

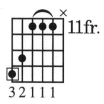

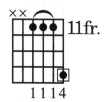

G♭ minor

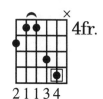

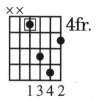

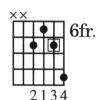

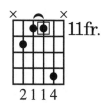

G♭ dominant 7

1 3 1 2 1 1

2fr.

1 3 1 2 4 1

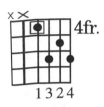

4fr.

1 3 2 4

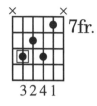

7fr.

3 2 4 1

9fr.

1 3 1 4 1

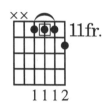

11fr.

1 1 1 2

G♭ major 7

1 3 4 2

4 3 2 1

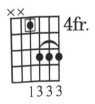

4fr.

1 3 3 3

6fr.

4 3 1 1 1

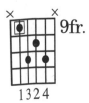

9fr.

1 3 2 4

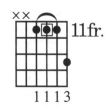

11fr.

1 1 1 3

G♭ minor 7

1 3 1 1 1 1

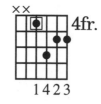

4fr.

1 4 2 3

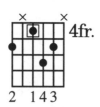

4fr.

2   1 4 3

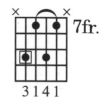

7fr.

3 1 4 1

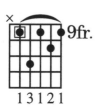

9fr.

1 3 1 2 1

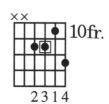

10fr.

2 3 1 4

G♭9

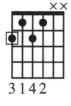

3 1 4 2

1 3 1 2 1 4

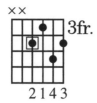

3fr.

2 1 4 3

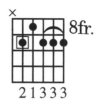

8fr.

2 1 3 3 3

G♭13

1 3 1 2 4 1

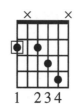

1   2 3 4

(G♭13)

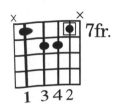 7fr.

1 3 4 2

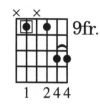 9fr.

1 2 4 4

G♭6

3 2 4 1

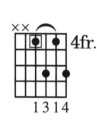 4fr.

1 3 1 4

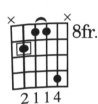 8fr.

2 1 1 4

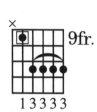 9fr.

1 3 3 3 3

G♭ sus

1 2 3 4 1 1

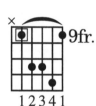 9fr.

1 2 3 4 1

G♭ augmented

 3fr.

3 2 1 1

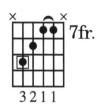 7fr.

3 2 1 1

G♭ diminished 7

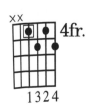 4fr.

1 3 2 4

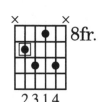 8fr.

2 3 1 4

Key of G

G major

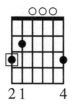

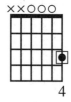

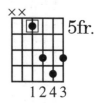

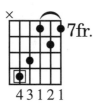

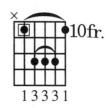

G minor

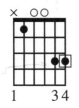

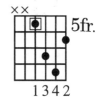

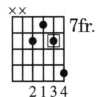

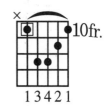

G dominant 7

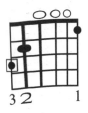 

 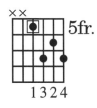

G major 7

 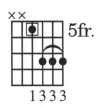

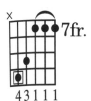 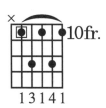

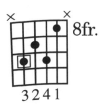 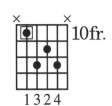

G minor 7

 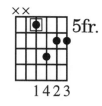

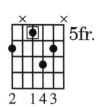 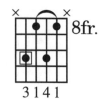

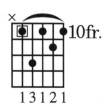 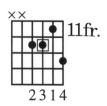

G9

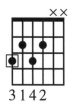 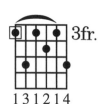

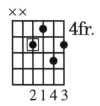 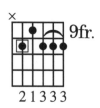

G13

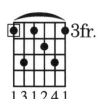 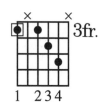

(G13)

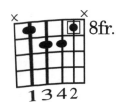 8fr.

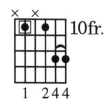 10fr.

G6

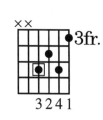 3fr.

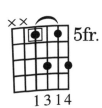 5fr.

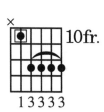 10fr.

G sus

 3fr.

G augmented

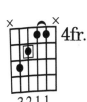 4fr.

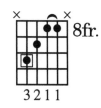 8fr.

G diminished 7

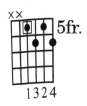 5fr.

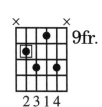 9fr.

39

Key of A♭

A♭ major

43111

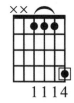
1114

4fr.
13421 1

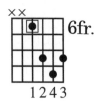
6fr.
1243

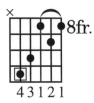
8fr.
43121

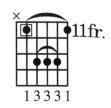
11fr.
13331

A♭ minor

4fr.
134111

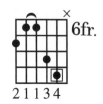
6fr.
21134

6fr.
1342

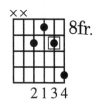
8fr.
2134

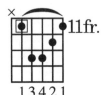
11fr.
13421

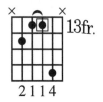
13fr.
2114

A♭ dominant 7

1 1 1 2

4fr.

1 3 1 2 1 1

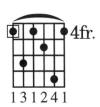

4fr.

1 3 1 2 4 1

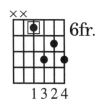

6fr.

1 3 2 4

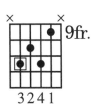

9fr.

3 2 4 1

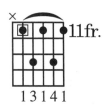

11fr.

1 3 1 4 1

A♭ major 7

1 1 1 3

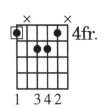

4fr.

1 3 4 2

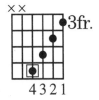

3fr.

4 3 2 1

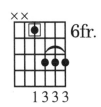

6fr.

1 3 3 3

8fr.

4 3 1 1 1

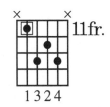

11fr.

1 3 2 4

A♭ minor 7

4fr.

1 3 1 1 1 1

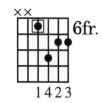

6fr.

1 4 2 3

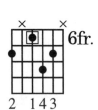

6fr.

2 1 4 3

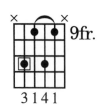

9fr.

3 1 4 1

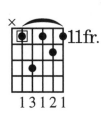

11fr.

1 3 1 2 1

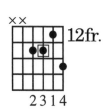

12fr.

2 3 1 4

A♭9

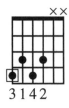

3 1 4 2

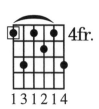

4fr.

1 3 1 2 1 4

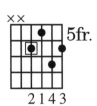

5fr.

2 1 4 3

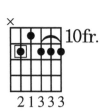

10fr.

2 1 3 3 3

A♭13

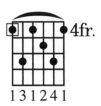

4fr.

1 3 1 2 4 1

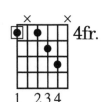

4fr.

1 2 3 4

(A♭13)

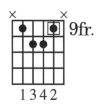 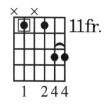

A♭6

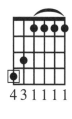 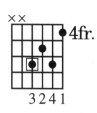

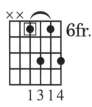 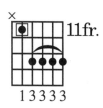

A♭ sus

A♭ augmented

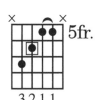 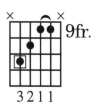

A♭ diminished 7

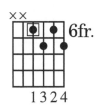 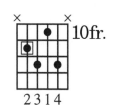

Key of A

A major

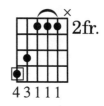

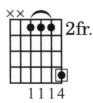

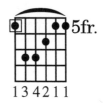

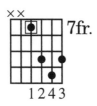

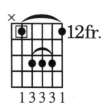

A minor

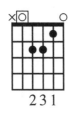

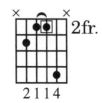

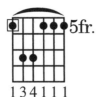

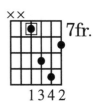

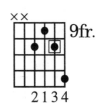

A dominant 7

 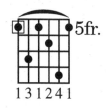

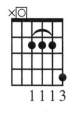 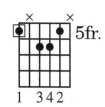

A major 7

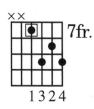 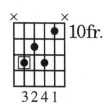

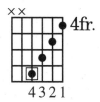 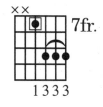

 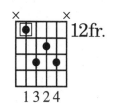

A minor 7

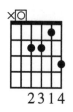

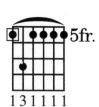
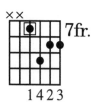

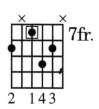
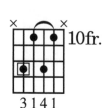

A9

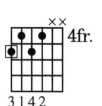

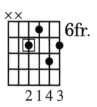
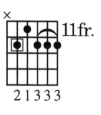

A13

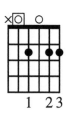
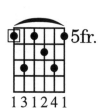

(A13)

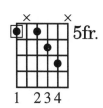 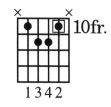

A6

 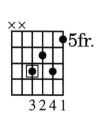

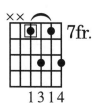 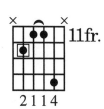

A sus

 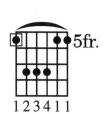

A augmented

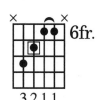 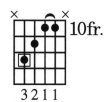

A diminished 7

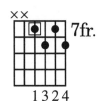 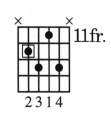

Key of B♭

B♭ major

1 3 3 3 1

3fr.
3 2 1 1 1 4

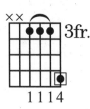
3fr.
1 1 1 4

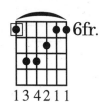
6fr.
1 3 4 2 1 1

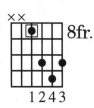
8fr.
1 2 4 3

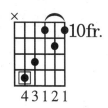
10fr.
4 3 1 2 1

B♭ minor

1 3 4 2 1

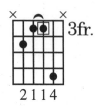
3fr.
2 1 1 4

6fr.
1 3 4 1 1 1

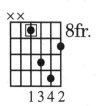
8fr.
1 3 4 2

8fr.
2 1 1 3 4

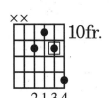
10fr.
2 1 3 4

Bb dominant 7

1 3 1 4 1

1 1 1 2

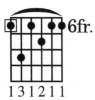

6fr.

1 3 1 2 1 1

6fr.

1 3 1 2 4 1

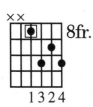

8fr.

1 3 2 4

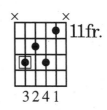

11fr.

3 2 4 1

Bb major 7

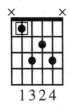

1 3 2 4

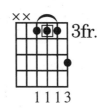

3fr.

1 1 1 3

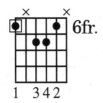

6fr.

1   3 4 2

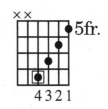

5fr.

4 3 2 1

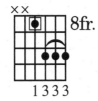

8fr.

1 3 3 3

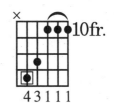

10fr.

4 3 1 1 1

49

B♭ minor 7

13121

2314

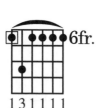
6fr.
131111

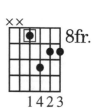
8fr.
1423

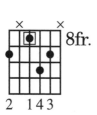
8fr.
2 143

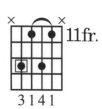
11fr.
3141

B♭9

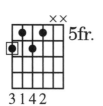
5fr.
3142

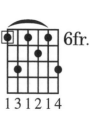
6fr.
131214

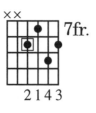
7fr.
2143

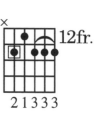
12fr.
21333

B♭13

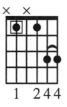
1 244

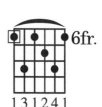
6fr.
131241

50

(B♭13)

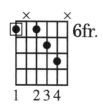 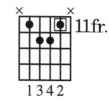

B♭6

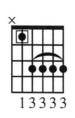 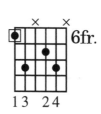

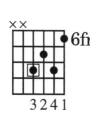 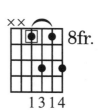

B♭ sus

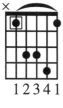 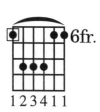

B♭ augmented

 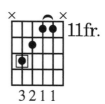

B♭ diminished 7

 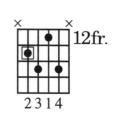

51

Key of B

B major

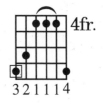

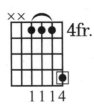

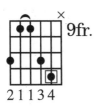

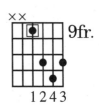

B minor

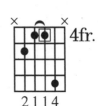

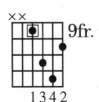

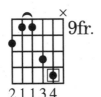

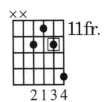

B dominant 7

2 1 3 4

1 3 1 4 1

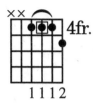

1 1 1 2

1 3 1 2 1 1

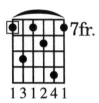

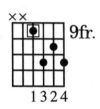

1 3 1 2 4 1

1 3 2 4

B major 7

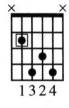

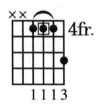

1 3 2 4

1 1 1 3

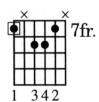

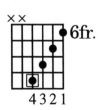

1   3 4 2

4 3 2 1

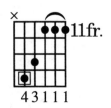

1 3 3 3

4 3 1 1 1

B minor 7

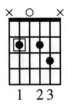

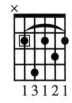

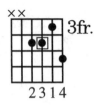

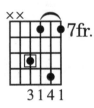

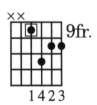

B9

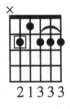

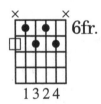

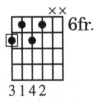

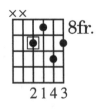

B13

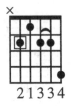

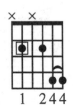

(B13)

 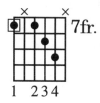

B6

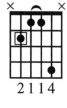 

 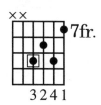

B sus

 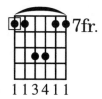

B augmented

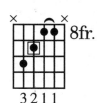 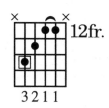

B diminished 7

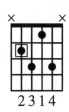 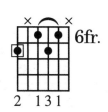

GUITAR TAB GLOSSARY
Tablature Explanation

Reading Tablature: Tablature illustrates the six strings of the guitar. Notes and chords are indicated by the placement of fret numbers on a given string(s).

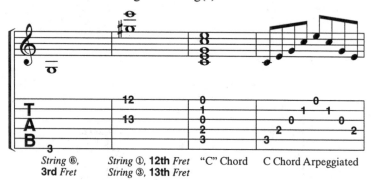

String ⑥,   String ①, **12th** *Fret*   "C" Chord   C Chord Arpeggiated
3rd *Fret*   String ③, **13th** *Fret*

Bending Notes

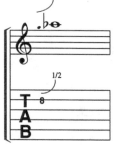

Half Step: Play the note and bend the string one half step.

Whole Step: Play the note and bend the string one whole step.

Prebend and Release: Bend the string, play it, then release to the original note.

Articulations

Hammer On: Play lower note, then "hammer on" to higher note with another finger. Only the first note is attacked.

Pull Off: Play higher note, then "pull off" to lower note with another finger. Only the first note is attacked.

Legato Slide: Play note and slide to the following note. (Only first note is attacked.)

Rhythm Notation

Strum Indications: Strum with indicated rhythm. The chord voicings are found on the first page of the transcription underneath the song title.